What You Need to Know Before You Go

What You Need to Know Before You Go

A GUIDE TO FLORIDA ESTATE PLANNING, PROBATE, AND MEDICAID

Gregory Ebenfeld, Esq.

© 2018 Gregory Ebenfeld
All rights reserved.

Please note that tax, estate planning, probate, and Medicaid laws change frequently, and this book is not intended to give specific legal advice. Please contact an attorney of your own choosing to discuss the circumstances of your family's situation.

ISBN-13: 9781979792684
ISBN-10: 1979792682
Library of Congress Control Number: 2017917835
CreateSpace Independent Publishing Platform
North Charleston, South Carolina

Table of Contents

Overview · ix

About the Author · xi

Acknowledgments · xiii

The Need for Estate Planning · 1

Last Will and Testament · 4

Without a Valid Will, You Will Be Unable To · · · · · · · · · · · · · 6

The Advantages of Having a Valid Last Will and Testament · · · · · · 8

Provisions Every Florida Last Will and Testament Should Have · · 10

Determining Domicile · 12

Establishing Florida Domicile · 14

What Happens to Your Assets When You Die · · · · · · · · · · · · · 17

The Superdeed · 21

Other Ways to Avoid the Probate Process · · · · · · · · · · · · · · · 25

A Revocable Living Trust · 32

How a Revocable Living Trust Works · · · · · · · · · · · · · · · · · · 34

The Advantages of a Revocable Living Trust · · · · · · · · · · · · · · 36

The Plan for the Healthy · 39

The Plan for the Healthy Thirty- to Sixty-Year-Old · · · · · · · · · 43

Newly Married · 44

Newly Married with Minor Children · · · · · · · · · · · · · · · · · · 46

Married With Newly Adult Children · · · · · · · · · · · · · · · · · · 49

Married With Adult Children · 51

Older Married Couples with Adult Children · · · · · · · · · · · · · · 54

Married with a Sick Spouse · 56

Medicaid Planning · 57

Other Medicaid Qualifications · 60

Qualified Income Trust · 61

Personal-Services Contract · 64

How the Calculation of the Funds Sheltered Is Determined · · · · 65

Who Should Sign the Personal-Services Contract · · · · · · · · · · · 66

Frequently Asked by Seniors · 69

Florida Homestead · 73

Changing Family Dynamics (Second Marriages) · · · · · · · · · · · · 79

Elective Share Issues · 83

Costs · 86

Conclusion · 89

Glossary · 91

Overview

I have written this book to help you understand the need to plan for different contingencies in life and to provide an understanding about legal issues that may impact those contingencies. It is my hope that reading this book will increase your awareness and provide a call to action.

Over the course of this book, I will give you an idea of the estate planning process in the different stages of your life. As much as we would like to think that doing estate and life planning is a one-time occurrence, it is not. Your goals for your estate plan will be different as you age. To think that a twenty-year-old's estate plan is the same as a seventy-five-year-old's is unrealistic.

Throughout this book, I will share personal experiences about how my clients have changed their estate plans over time to give you some ideas about how your estate plan may be structured.

It is my experience that, when a person reaches about twenty-three years of age, he or she begins to contemplate his or her own mortality. At first, it may be a fleeting thought. Maybe a friend or grandparent has passed away, and the thought of death starts to invade the realm of consciousness. It is not until a person gets married or perhaps starts having children that he or she really thinks about the following questions:

- If I die, who will take care of my kids?
- Who will take care of paying their expenses?
- Should I direct how things should be taken care of?

Even though this person knows that these questions should be addressed, it usually takes a few more years until he or she begins to do something about it.

About the Author

Gregory Ebenfeld, Esq. opened his law practice in Hollywood, Florida, in 1995 after attaining his master of laws in taxation (LLM) from the University of Florida College of Law. He earned his law degree (JD) from Ohio Northern University Law School and his undergraduate degree (BS) in finance from Albright College.

Mr. Ebenfeld was admitted to the Florida Bar in 1992. He is active in community affairs. He is a member of the Real Property, Probate, and Trust Law Section of the Florida Bar and a member of the Elder Law Section of the Florida Bar. Mr. Ebenfeld also served as president of the North Dade South Broward Estate Planning Council. He has consistently achieved an AV rating by Martindale-Hubbell—the highest rating an attorney can achieve.

Mr. Ebenfeld has been a guest speaker on several radio talk shows, including *Financial Talk* on WPBR 1340 AM, *Creative Estate Planning* on WSBR 740 AM, and *Legal Club Live* on WAXY 790 AM. He regularly leads estate planning seminars.

In his spare time, Mr. Ebenfeld has also achieved a black belt in USA Goju Federation Karate and donates his time to teach children karate two nights a week. He is married to Cindy Ebenfeld, also an attorney, and they have one adult son, Zachary. They reside in Pembroke Pines, Florida.

Acknowledgments

I would like to thank the following people who helped me complete this book: My beautiful and devoted wife, Cindy Ebenfeld, who poured over manuscripts with me; my legal assistant, Melody Bucher; my brother and unofficial editor, Wayne Ebenfeld; and my office mate and fellow tax attorney and contributing editor, Joseph Schimmel.

I would also like to thank Natalee Ryan, who supplied all the illustrations for this book. Natalee grew up in Upstate New York and is pursuing an education in information technology and web science at Rensselaer Polytechnic Institute.

The Need for Estate Planning

Everyone knows something must be done; too few act responsibly. From the time the Egyptian pyramids were built, people have planned for their deaths. Through the ages, even the old cliché from founding father Benjamin Franklin rings true today: "The only thing certain is death and taxes." Although we cannot avoid death, we can plan for it. Estate planning is for people who have acquired even a small amount of wealth throughout their lives and would like this capital to pass on to their surviving family with the fewest problems, financial and otherwise.

Estate planning is not always needed. For example, several years ago a young man in his early twenties came to my office for what he thought was to seek estate planning advice. He related to me that he had no spouse, significant other, children, parents, or real friends and did not have anyone he particularly cared for or any charity he supported. He told me that he had not done any estate planning and mistakenly thought this was something he needed.

I then asked him about his goals in life. He said that his only objective was to spend all his money before he died. He did not care what would happen to him or his affairs after his death. I advised him that maybe in the future, his circumstances would change, but for right now, all he really needed was investment and income planning, *not* estate planning. I suggested he should employ the services of an investment adviser.

For the majority of people, this is not the case. Most people have family members, friends, or charities that are important to them and whom they would want to receive their property if something were to happen. Or even if they have no assets, they have certain people they would want to make medical decisions for them if they could not. This book is for those people and others who may not need estate planning at the present time but would like to understand more about estate planning to use in the future.

Before suggesting any type of planning, I believe it is important to explain what happens to the estates of people who die without doing any planning whatsoever.

In the case of a person dying without a last will and testament or other documents, the state in which the deceased person lived (domiciled) will do the estate planning for him or her. When a person dies without a valid last will and testament, the state calls this dying "intestate." In effect, the state writes the person's last will and testament and distributes all the person's assets according to the current state law. When a person dies intestate, his or her assets are distributed according to state law (statute), which in most cases is not how the deceased person would have wanted his or her wealth to be distributed.

The following few pages describe how the Florida probate court (the court that governs the distribution of assets when a person dies with or without a last will and testament) would distribute a person's assets if a person were to die without a properly drafted last will and testament.

Last Will and Testament

Based on Florida Intestate Statute, Chapter 732
First: The probate judge shall determine who will serve as administrator of my estate, but preference may be given to

a) my surviving spouse,
b) the person selected by a majority in interest of my heirs, or
c) my heir nearest in degree.

If more than one applies, the court may exercise its discretion in selecting the one best qualified for the office.

Second: All my assets shall be converted to cash, and all my debts will be paid, including taxes, probate fees, administrative fees, and attorney's fees.

Third: If my spouse and I have children, then my spouse shall inherit the entire estate. If I had children from another partner, then half of my assets would be paid to my spouse, and the rest would be divided and paid equally to my children.

Fourth: If my children are minors (under the age of eighteen) at the time of my death, then a guardian shall be appointed. The guardian need not be my spouse or my children's surviving parent.

Fifth: When my children reach age eighteen, all their inheritance shall be paid directly to them, regardless of their financial or emotional maturity.

Sixth: If none of my children survives me or if I have no children, the remainder of my assets shall be distributed outright to my parents, if living. Otherwise, it will be distributed to my brothers and sisters or their heirs.

Seventh: If I am not survived by my spouse, children, or parents, the probate court shall seek out my closest blood relatives and divide my estate among them in a way that gives equal shares to my closest relatives or their descendants.

Eighth: If no relatives can be located, then all my property goes to the state.

Without a Valid Will, You Will Be Unable To

1. Select the person who will administer your estate;
2. Select the guardian of your children (if a preneed guardianship document has not been signed);
3. Waive the need for a bond;
4. Choose the person you would want to continue your business; or
5. Make specific bequests or create testamentary trusts.

Most people want to avoid these adverse effects by having a valid will.

I encountered the following situation with one of my clients. About ten years ago, Amy came into my office and told me that she had been living with her boyfriend, Danny (whom she referred to as her spouse), for thirty years. She affirmed that they shared everything.

Early in their relationship, she did not have good credit, and they had purchased the home they shared in Danny's name. Danny had made all the payments. When Danny died unexpectedly, Amy came into my office to see how she could sell the house and move. I asked her if Danny had a last will and testament, but he did not. I then asked if Danny had any children, to which she also said no. I asked if he had any siblings, and she said he had a brother, but they were estranged and had not spoken to him in many years.

Unfortunately, despite Danny's likely desire that Amy would have his house, I told her that his brother would be inheriting the house. And since she was not legally married and Danny did not have a will, she would not be inheriting anything. This was a sad situation that could have been avoided very easily if Danny had done some simple estate planning.

Unfortunately, this situation is not all that uncommon, and many families have come to my office too late to do any effective estate planning.

So who should prepare your last will and testament? I believe it is very important to have an attorney draw up a last will and testament. Only an attorney can give you the proper advice as to the laws under the state where you live. Many people have come to my office with a form last will and testament that they found online or got from an office supply store. There have been many times when the last wills and testaments have not been filled out or signed properly, and they are not worth the paper they are written on. I believe that, for a few hundred dollars, it is well worth the peace of mind to know that the last will and testament is correctly done.

The Advantages of Having a Valid Last Will and Testament

Despite the widespread use of a revocable trust (which I will discuss in detail later) or joint ownership as a substitute for a last will and testament, the last will and testament remains a valuable estate planning tool. A valid will serves several purposes that revocable trusts and other estate planning tools cannot. Only a valid will can appoint a personal representative of your estate. This person will do things such as sell a property and represent the estate in a wrongful death claim. In addition, a valid last will and testament will allow you to appoint a guardian for your minor children (if you did not designate a preneed guardianship).

For a will to be fully effective in Florida, it must meet the following criteria:

1. Qualify for admission to probate. This means the testator (the person who the will belongs to) must sign the document at the end. In addition, it must be signed in the presence of two witnesses, who also sign.

2. Express the testator's decisions so clearly that court proceedings are not required to determine its meaning.
3. Avoid violation of the Rule against Perpetuities (which states that the distribution to beneficiaries must occur within 360 years) and other rules.

Far too many wills fail to achieve one or more of these requirements, which often results in expensive probate costs and litigation and could lead to a distribution of the person's assets in a way that would not conform to his or her wishes.

Provisions Every Florida Last Will and Testament Should Have

1. Identify the testator (creator of the document).
2. Revoke all previous last will and testaments and codicils (an amendment to a last will and testament), and declare the instrument to be the testator's last will and testament.
3. Name a personal representative and require this person to pay any debts, funeral costs, and expenses of administration with estate proceeds.
4. Grant powers to the personal representative to sell real estate, avoid posting a bond, and be compensated, if warranted.
5. Specify who will receive all tangible personal property.
   a. Florida law allows a separate writing to dispose tangible personal property. The testator must sign this separate writing, along with describe the items and beneficiaries with reasonable certainty. And the testator must refer to this separate writing in the will.
6. Include a residuary clause, which gives the remainder of one's estate to a specific person, trust, or charity.

a. When a residuary clause leaves the rest of a person's estate to a revocable living trust, pour-over provisions must be included. These provisions fund the trust with assets "poured over" from the last will and testament. A last will and testament with these provisions is often called a "pour-over will."
7. Name contingent beneficiaries who will only receive the property if the initial beneficiary predeceases the testator.
8. Designate guardians for minor children.
9. Include a simultaneous death clause that provides for the disposition of the testator's estate if the testator and a beneficiary should die at the same time.

In Florida, the testator must sign his or her name at the end of the last will and testament. The last will and testament should also have page numbers. There must be at least two witnesses, who must sign in each other's presence and in the presence of the testator.

The last will and testament should also include a self-proving affidavit. A notary must be present to attest to the signatures of the testator and witnesses. If the signatures are not notarized, stringent requirements make sure the last will and testament is valid. Some of these rules require that, after the testator's death, the witnesses must sign an affidavit stating that they had viewed the signing of the last will and testament. It is prudent to have the last will and testament self-proving to avoid the court requiring further authentication.

Determining Domicile

Determining the domicile (legal residence) of the testator is very important. At the time of death, the testator's domicile determines within which state and county the will is probated.

A person can have many residences but only one domicile. The determination of a person's domicile is very important even when a person dies. Each state where a person has a residence will want to have that person domiciled in that state in order to probate (and possibly tax) all the person's assets. Anyone who has residences in two or more states faces a domicile problem.

Why should a person become a resident and declare domicile in the state of Florida? The State of Florida has a constitutional prohibition against Florida estate tax being levied against the estates of Florida domiciliaries. Many other states—such as Connecticut, Massachusetts, New Jersey, and New York—do impose a substantial estate tax. If you are now domiciled in one of the states that have taxes and you become a Florida domiciliary, eliminating the state tax will reduce your total tax burden.

How does someone establish a Florida domicile? Persons from other states who wish to establish Florida as their legal place of domicile can do so by forming an intent and doing some overt acts to establish a Florida domicile.

Establishing Florida Domicile

1. File a Florida Declaration of Domicile, pursuant to Section 222.17 of the Florida Statutes. Forms are available at the offices of the clerk of the circuit court in every county.
2. File for a homestead exemption on your Florida residence (if you own your residence), and cancel any homestead filing in other states.
3. Register to vote in Florida, and vote in Florida. (And unregister elsewhere.)
4. Have a Florida driver's license, and give up all out-of-state driver's licenses.
5. Transfer the title to your personal automobiles to Florida, and obtain Florida license plates.
6. Execute a new last will and testament reflecting Florida as your place of residence.
7. File federal income tax returns showing your Florida address.
8. If appropriate, file a nonresident income tax return in your former state of residence.

WHAT YOU NEED TO KNOW BEFORE YOU GO

9. Open Florida bank and other financial accounts, and close all bank and other financial accounts, including brokerage accounts, in other jurisdictions. Close safe deposit boxes in other jurisdictions, and, if appropriate, rent a safe deposit box in Florida.
10. Register a change of address with all creditors, including credit card issuers.
11. Change your passport address to reflect your Florida residence.
12. Affiliate with a church or synagogue in Florida.
13. Affiliate with fraternal or social organizations in Florida, and disaffiliate with similar organizations in your prior state of residence.
14. Transfer as much tangible personal property as feasible, particularly expensive property, to Florida.
15. Consider selling any real property you own in other jurisdictions.
16. Consider selling business interests in other jurisdictions or, if feasible, placing those interests in a trust having a Florida situs.
17. Acquire cemetery plots in Florida.

Doing all of the above is not necessarily required, and though all these things may be in place, your prior state of residence may still challenge your change of domicile. If you wish to establish and document Florida domicile, you should do as many of the above items as feasible.

Many people will spend substantial periods of time in other states. This time is not determinative of domicile. Even if Florida domicile is established, you can be subject to tax in another jurisdiction if you own real property located outside Florida.

What Happens to Your Assets When You Die

What actually happens when you die with a properly drawn last will and testament? The first step is to determine what, if any, of the assets that need to go through the probate process. In the state of Florida, an attorney must be hired to handle the administration of your probate estate. Once the attorney is hired, he or she submits your last will and testament to the probate court so the court can determine if it meets the test of a valid last will and testament. When the court determines that the last will and testament is legal in form and was properly executed, the court will accept it for probate.

The attorney also submits paper work to appoint a personal representative of the probate estate. (This is known as the executor in other states.) The personal representative must meet certain requirements. He or she should

1. be over the age of eighteen,
2. not be a convicted felon, and
3. either reside in the state of Florida or be your blood relative or spouse of a blood relative.

Once the court determines that the personal representative meets these requirements, the court will grant that person the right to be the personal representative and will issue letters of administration, allowing the personal representative to act on behalf of the estate.

This can take the court several months to grant. The personal representative of your estate must make sure that all your wishes, as outlined in your will, are carried out. The personal representative presents the probate court with a list of the assets and liabilities of your estate. A legal notice is subsequently published in a local newspaper. Potential beneficiaries of your estate can challenge the validity of your last will and testament.

Next, the court will hear any objections to your will and rule on their validity. If the terms of the last will and testament are unclear, the court will interpret the terms and decide what you meant.

Your legal residence determines which probate court has proper jurisdiction over your assets. If you have your legal residence in Florida but own real estate in other states, unless a revocable living trust was used, the probate court of each state must be used to probate the real estate in that state. This is called "ancillary administration." This means that an attorney may need to be hired in every state that real estate is located.

The probate process is very time consuming, anywhere from one to five years or more if anyone contests the last will and testament or other parts of the probate process. The beneficiaries must wait until the probate process is complete before they receive their complete inheritance, although sometimes the court will allow a partial distribution of an inheritance before the probate process has been completed. A family allowance may be used to help spouses and minor children have money to live during the probate process.

The probate process is not a private matter. If a person is known to the community or if there is anything unusual about the size or nature of his or her estate, the newspaper is free to print the details. At this point, unscrupulous persons may come out of the woodwork.

I recall a fellow attorney telling me about one of his client's encounters. A woman in her midseventies had just lost her husband. During their fifty-three years of marriage, her husband had taken care of all the financial affairs. A couple of weeks after her husband's death, a person came to her door and notified her that he was a roofer and that her husband had contracted with him to redo their roof. He showed her what seemed to be a legal contract with what looked like her husband's signature. The man requested that she pay him $5,000, which would be half of the contract price.

She paid the $5,000 and never heard from him again. When the man was finally caught, he bragged that he would look in the obituaries to find a person's name and then look up the will in the public records. He would then copy the signature from the will and bring a phony contract to the grieving widow.

In the state of Florida, there are two types of probate administration: summary and formal. A summary administration can only be done if the assets in your estate are under $75,000 or if you have been deceased for more than two years. This administration is typically a lot quicker than the formal administration and can usually be completed in about six to nine months. On the other hand, a formal administration is for estates worth more than $75,000 and can take upward of one year even for a standard administration.

Probate administration is very costly. When all fees and costs are added up, the cost of probate can easily be several thousand dollars. A good rule of thumb is that the total cost of administration will be about 6 to 15 percent of the assets going through the probate process.

The Superdeed

If you don't want to go through probate, what can you do? There are several ways to avoid the probate process, and I will discuss some of them, but one asset in particular can be dealt with differently from all the rest. Many of my clients come to my office looking to avoid the probate process, but typically their estates consist solely of their Florida primary home (homestead property). I have created a method in which a person can give real property to his or her beneficiaries without going through the probate process. I call this method a "superdeed."

This method will enable you to

- distribute your property at death to your heirs;
- save thousands of dollars in the probate process;
- keep control of your property during your lifetime;
- retain the power to sell your property without your heirs being required to sign the deed;
- change the recipients of your property at any time; and
- retain your homestead exemption.

Most people work their entire lives to own a home free and clear of a mortgage, but what they don't realize is that, at their death, this asset would have to go through the probate process in order to be distributed to their heirs.

In order to use the superdeed, a person must first own a piece of property in his or her own name, which should be free and clear of mortgage. If the property does have a mortgage, then the mortgage company should be contacted to allow for the new deed. Many practitioners use what is called a life estate deed with a remainder interest to children to transfer property at the death of the individual to their heirs without going through the probate process. The life estate deed grants the owner of the property the ability to retain all rights and live there for his or her lifetime, and only upon his or her death does the property pass to the heirs identified in the deed.

There can be several problems with the life estate deed. In the traditional life estate deed, the property owner is forbidden to sell the property without the consent of his or her heirs, and he or she cannot change the beneficiaries or mortgage the property without the signature of all people included in the deed.

Usually a traditional life estate deed is not the best way to transfer your property at death without probate. The superdeed allows you to transfer your property at death without going through probate. It also allows you to keep complete control over the property during your lifetime. With the superdeed, you also retain the power to sell the property without your heirs' consent, and you can change the person's set to receive your property anytime you choose. Moreover, within the state of Florida, if your home is transferred via the superdeed, you retain your homestead exemption on the property.

For example, Jerry came into my office and told me that he had bought his home in Pembroke Pines in Broward County, Florida, over thirty years ago for $55,000. He paid off any mortgage he had and owned his home outright. Jerry had two children, Hank and Mark. Jerry had a very small estate. All he owned was his home, now worth $275,000, and a small bank account worth $5,500. Upon his death, he wanted his home to be split fifty-fifty between his two children without going through the hassle and expense of probate. I told him we could set up the superdeed to avoid probate. We made a superdeed, which he signed, and we had it recorded with the Broward County Court.

Unfortunately, Jerry died three years later. His children contacted me to ask what needed to be done. I told them they needed to record the death certificate in Broward County, and then the house belonged to them. Not only were they able to sell the house for $300,000 and pay no capital-gains taxes, they were also able to avoid probate. The ease and simplicity of the superdeed process enabled Jerry's grieving family to avoid the expense and time-consuming probate process.

Other Ways to Avoid the Probate Process

After looking at the wasted time and money associated with the probate process, you should note that several ways to avoid probate exist. I will explain five other ways to avoid the probate process.

Joint Tenancy

Joint tenancy is a common ownership arrangement in which two or more people hold title to property. This form of ownership avoids probate because title automatically passes to the surviving owners upon the death of a joint owner. This automatic transfer is called a right of survivorship. At first glance, placing all your assets into joint tenancy would seem like a great idea; however, many problems can arise with this arrangement. The initial transfer of the property into joint tenancy brings up a possible gift-tax situation, (the tax on gifts over $15,000 in 2018) if the property is transferred into joint tenancy with a person who is not your spouse.

When a person dies owning property in only his or her name, the income tax law allows the property to be passed on to the beneficiary with the basis stepped up to fair market value. This gives the beneficiary the opportunity to sell the property immediately without having to pay capital gains tax. If the property is in joint names, only a portion of the property may qualify for the step up in basis.

Furthermore, even though probate is avoided at the first death, the property must go through probate at the second death. The property must also go through probate if all joint tenants happen to die in a common disaster.

There can also be unintended consequences of putting assets in joint tenancy with rights of survivorship. This happened to Marsha. Marsha had a very small estate. She had a house and bank account worth about $100,000 each. Marsha was getting older, and she thought it was about time she did some estate planning. She had two daughters: Samantha, who lived in Florida near Marsha, and Donna, who lived in Texas. Marsha went to her lawyer, who specialized in real estate, and told him to make her a last will and testament. She said she wanted everything to be split evenly between her two daughters. The real-estate attorney created a will for her that gave everything evenly to her two daughters.

Because Marsha knew she was getting older and did not want to write checks anymore, she added Samantha on her bank account as a joint tenant. Five years later, Marsha died, and Samantha and Donna were not on the greatest of terms. Since Samantha was on the bank account with her mother, she transferred it into her own bank account, while the house, her only other asset, went through probate and was then divided evenly between Samantha and Donna. Donna ended up with half the home worth (about $50,000), and Samantha ended up with other half of the home, plus the bank account (worth about $100,000).

This is not what Marsha had intended. Even if Marsha had put both Samantha and Donna on the bank account, it may not have solved the problem. The first of the daughters to go to the bank could still have withdrawn the entire bank account.

POD—In Trust for Accounts

If you have a bank account, you can have it titled "Payable on Death" or "POD." If you have a brokerage account, it will be called "Transfer on Death" or "TOD" account. "In Trust For" or "Transfer on Death" accounts allow you to put a beneficiary on your accounts so that, upon your death, the beneficiary gives the broker or bank a death certificate and receives the asset.

This is a good probate avoidance technique if all you have is a bank account; however, there are some problems with these types of accounts. One potential problem is that, during the lifetime of the account owner, he or she is the only person who has access to the account. This becomes a problem if the person whose name is on the account owner becomes mentally disabled because no one has the power to pay bills from this account or to make any changes to the investments if a new and better investment becomes available.

Another potential problem arises if the beneficiary dies and there are no other beneficiaries on the account. This will lead to a probate administration of the account. Problems can also arise if the beneficiary of the account is a minor, because a minor cannot own sums larger than $15,000 without a guardianship.

Lifetime Gifts

Any gifts made during life will avoid probate, even if these gifts are made on a person's deathbed. Any gifts of property carry over the original owner's basis to the beneficiary. Outright distribution of assets is usually not a good idea for estate planning purposes because, although the assets are out of your estate, the beneficiary loses the ability to increase his or her basis upon death (step up in basis) if the beneficiary were to receive the assets by last will and testament or trust.

For a gift to avoid probate, either it must be in a trust, or the owner must relinquish all rights over the property. Most people are understandably reluctant to give away total control over a gift during their lifetime. Also, if a gift of over $15,000 is made, a single recipient must file a Form 709 with the IRS. Also, any gift given within five years will be subject to the look-back period for Medicaid qualification. This will be examined later.

You should be very wary of giving gifts of property just to avoid probate, as the following example shows. Victor was ninety-five years old and had two sons, Harvey and Steven. He owned a valuable rental home, which he bought in 1940 for $35,000, $5,000 of which was allocated to the land. The home was now worth $1 million. Victor knew his health was failing, and he did not want the rental home to go through a lengthy probate process. He gifted the rental home to his two sons via a quit claim deed.

About six months after the gift, Victor died. Harvey and Steven then sold the property for $1 million. When Victor's sons sold the property, they incurred a capital gains tax of approximately $149,000. This is calculated by taking the selling price of $1 million and subtracting the basis. The original cost of the property was $35,000, but since it had been a rental property, the building was fully depreciated, and the remaining basis was $5,000 (the land). They had to pay capital gains tax on $995,000, at 15 percent, based on 2016 tax rates, totaling $150,000 in taxes, plus potentially investment income tax, which could bring the rate close to 25 percent.

If Victor had held the property until his death and distributed the property through his last will and testament, then the property would have had a step up in basis, and Harvey and Steven would not have had to pay any capital gains taxes. Even if they had paid probate fees, which could have been $40,000 or $60,000, it would still have been cheaper than paying the capital gains tax. Before you make any major gifts, please see a qualified attorney or CPA so you can get the best advice as to how to transfer these assets based on the various tax consequences.

Life Insurance

Under normal circumstances, life insurance is not subject to probate administration if the beneficiary is anyone other than the insured's estate. It is very important that you make sure you have a named beneficiary for your life insurance contract. For couples with small children, life insurance can be tricky. What I have seen many times is that a couple has life insurance on the spouse who makes the most money. The beneficiary of the life insurance is the spouse first and then the children. While this sounds like a good plan, many problems may exist.

The following example illustrates potential problems with this scenario. Jimmy and Ellen were married and had two small children, Jane and Robert. Both Jimmy and Ellen worked, and each had life insurance policies for the sum of $500,000. Their contract with the life insurance company stated that the beneficiary of each policy fell to each other, and the secondary beneficiaries were the children.

Sadly, while driving home from vacation one year without the children, Jimmy and Ellen were killed in an auto accident. Because their children were minors and could not inherit the $1 million, a guardian was appointed for the children. Robert was the older of the children, and upon him reaching the age of eighteen, he received $500,000. Feeling that he had just won the lottery, he bought a very expensive car and went on a spending spree. Within two years, he had no money and essentially ended up living on the street.

Jane was two years behind Robert and received her $500,000 next. She was going to go to college, but with $500,000, she thought she would travel, have fun, see the world, and get her education later. Without the benefit of proper adult supervision, the two children were not capable of managing these financial accounts independently and could not appropriately prepare for securing their financial future in the manner that Jimmy and Ellen would have envisioned.

The moral of this story is that if Jimmy and Ellen had put the life insurance in a trust, they could have given the money to the children when they were older and more able to financially manage it. They could have made a last will and testament with testamentary trusts built in for the benefit of the children and made the trust the beneficiary of their life insurance and avoid probate.

Revocable Living Trusts

The best way to avoid probate is through a revocable living trust—a legal document that is considered a distinct legal entity created to hold ownership of an individual's assets. The revocable living trust is considered the best way to both avoid probate and control the disposition of one's assets upon death. The next section examines what a revocable living trust is, how it works, and what the advantages of having one are.

A Revocable Living Trust

A revocable living trust is a document that allows a person to hold assets as trustee. It is also considered a will substitute since it will allow a person to distribute the assets to beneficiaries after death. A revocable living trust does not die; therefore, the assets in the trust avoid probate. Many people fail to set up revocable living trusts because of misguided fears:

- Many believe they will have to give up control over the assets placed into the trust. Having a bank account in the name of a trust instead of their own names often puts people off.
- People think that revocable living trusts are much too complicated to understand.
- Many also believe that, once they place assets into the trust, they can never change the terms of the trust.

All these beliefs are incorrect. In a properly drafted revocable living trust, assets are placed into the trust (referred to as "funding the trust"). Whoever is named as the trustee of the revocable living trust has complete control over the disposition of the assets, which includes selling the assets, giving income to the person setting up the trust, and liquidating the trust.

The person setting up the trust is usually named as the trustee. By naming yourself as trustee, this keeps you in total control over the assets while you are competent to do so. If the trustee becomes disabled, a successor trustee can replace the trustee without the need for expensive guardianship proceedings.

Once the trust is correctly set up and funded, the person setting up the trust is free to deal with the trust property in the same manner as he or she dealt with the property prior to the trust's creation. The person setting up the trust also can retain the right to change the terms of the trust with the use of an amendment to the trust.

How a Revocable Living Trust Works

The revocable living trust eliminates the need for probate because, technically, the owner of the property is trustee of the revocable living trust and not the person who set up the trust. The trustee holds title to all the trust property. For example, bank accounts and real estate are titled "John Jones, Trustee to the John Jones Revocable Living Trust," but John Jones himself may possess, use, and enjoy the money and property to the same extent as he did before the trust was created.

The significance of not technically owning any of the assets in the trust becomes important upon your death. When you die, you technically own nothing; therefore, there is nothing to probate. If you are married, your surviving spouse can be your successor trustee. He or she would have the powers to sell, buy, or transfer property. Upon the death of your spouse, there would still be no probate because, again, all the assets would be in the trust and not in your spouse's name.

For the living trust to be effective, almost all your assets must be titled into the name of your living trust. Sometimes this is as easy as going to the bank and retitling the bank account. Sometimes this process is more difficult, requiring changing the title to property by using a deed.

The Advantages of a Revocable Living Trust

1. For the life of the person who sets up the revocable living trust, that individual may be the trustee, the manager of all the assets, and the beneficiary of the trust. When that person dies, having fully funded the trust, all the assets in the trust avoid the probate process.
2. The revocable living trust gives you complete control over your assets, allowing you to give whatever you wish to whomever you wish.
3. The revocable living trust also eliminates the personal representative's commissions. Since there is no need to have a probate administration, there is no need to have a personal representative appointed.
4. A pour-over will greatly reduce attorney's fees, and the time of receiving assets is almost immediate instead of waiting until the estate has been fully probated.
5. If you die leaving minor children, the revocable living trust eliminates the need for a court-appointed guardian to care

for your children's inherited property. Instead the successor trustee named in the trust will assume the responsibilities normally taken over by a guardian.

6. The revocable living trust keeps all your dispositive plans private, thus lessening the chances of unscrupulous people preying on those you leave behind.
7. Any property that you own in other states, if properly transferred to the trust, can avoid ancillary probate procedures, which is probate in another state.
8. If you run a family-owned business, the business can continue uninterrupted. The trustee is free to act as you would act. Your family does not have to wait for the probate process to end in order to sell or receive income from the business.
9. The revocable living trust requires no periodic trust reporting or accounting to the probate court since the court is not involved in the trust administration. An accounting is still required to the beneficiaries of the trust by the trustee of the trust.
10. No adverse income-tax consequences result from setting up the revocable living trust during your lifetime. The trust is not even required to file an income-tax return. All income and losses of your trust are reported on your individual federal and state tax returns.
11. A revocable living trust is inexpensive to establish. You maintain the trust yourself. You can transfer the assets into the trust yourself and save legal expenses.

12. The revocable living trust can be amended or revoked at any time during your lifetime.
13. You can also remove assets from the trust at any time.
14. If you become disabled or incapacitated, your successor trustee (the trustee appointed after the initial trustee) can immediately take over your affairs and manage your assets without the court's interference.

The Plan for the Healthy

People in their twenties and thirties typically do not embrace estate planning. Many are still single and reserve planning for when they are older and more established. They tend to live paycheck to paycheck and only engage in estate planning because their parents told them they need to have something in place just in case something happens. In many cases, their largest asset is the life insurance policy they receive from their employer. When they come into my office, I usually recommend doing a very basic estate plan, which usually includes a last will and testament, durable power of attorney for financial affairs, medical power of attorney, and a living will. In the next couple of chapters, I will go into further depth to explain these documents.

The last will and testament will instruct how property is to be distributed. The client usually gives the property to his or her siblings and parents. The durable power of attorney is also an important document. It is a legal document whereby one person (the principal) enables another person (the agent) to step into the principal's shoes and act on his or her behalf. Florida Statutes Chapter 709 allows this power to be granted to the agent until the principal dies or revokes the power. Many people mistakenly believe that the durable power of attorney survives death, which it does not. The moment the principal dies, the durable power of attorney no longer has any power. The durable power of attorney is also important to allow the agent to take care of the principal's interests if the principal is declared incapacitated.

In 2011, the Florida legislature changed the way durable powers of attorney should be written, and attorneys who practice estate planning subsequently had to change their documents. For example, with these changes, my durable power of attorney grew from a nine-page document to a more than twenty-page document. In this new document, the principal must affirmatively initial specific provisions in order for the provisions to be effective.

One of the most important provisions should be the ability for the agent to deal with Medicaid benefits, such as the ability to create an income trust and to create personal service agreements. I will spend a great deal of time discussing Medicaid benefits later. It is important to note that the durable power of attorney document is for financial matters.

Another document I highly recommend to a healthy person is a medical power of attorney, also called a designation of health care surrogate. The designation of health care surrogate and medical durable power of attorney are both similar to the durable power of attorney for property. The designation of health care surrogate allows you to give power to another to make certain health care decisions for you if you are incapacitated and unable to do so for yourself. This document should include a HIPAA Release. HIPAA refers to the Health Insurance Portability and Accountability Act of 1996, 42 USC 1320d, and 45 CFR 160-164. It is important to have this release in your health-care surrogate so the individual will be able to receive your health records and make an educated decision as to the best way in which you can get the medical procedures that would benefit you.

The last major document I recommend for the healthy person is a living will, sometimes considered a dying with dignity document. This document allows a doctor to remove life support apparatus if there is no hope of recovery. Signing this document may be difficult for individuals to address, but proper planning can make an enormous difference when tragedy strikes. It is widely known that medical breakthroughs in recent years have allowed people to live longer lives.

Unfortunately, sometimes elderly people become incapacitated and live for several years without hope for recovery. Many individuals faced with the possibility of living in a vegetative state would rather have their lives ended for them. The Florida legislature recognizes the living will as a medical directive allowing an individual to die when there is no hope of recovery. Without a proper directive, a hospital may be required to keep you in a vegetative state, causing tremendous costs and heartache to your family members.

In my documents, there is a three-prong test as to whether life support should be withdrawn: if the person is in a terminal condition, if the person is in an end-stage condition, and if the person is in a persistent vegetative state. I have the client decide whether he or she wants removal of nutrition and hydration (food and water).

Once these simple documents are in place, the twenty- to thirty-year-old should monitor whether these documents should be changed because of changes in his or her own life. Such changes would include marriage, divorce, children, death of his or her parents, or changes in the competency of people he or she has chosen to perform the duties of personal representative, agent, or health care surrogate.

The Plan for the Healthy Thirty- to Sixty-Year-Old

The plan for the healthy thirty- to sixty-year-old is usually very different from the twenty- to thirty-year-old. Major changes in the family structure usually happen at this time. People get married, divorced, have children, and need an estate plan that can change with the way their family changes.

Newly Married

Newly married couples should have an estate plan that includes a last will and testament. Sometimes this is called "I Love You Wills," because they state that, if something happens to one, then the other receives the entire estate. At this stage, I normally advise that if the couple has assets titled in joint names with rights of survivorship, they also should have their life insurance and retirement plans updated to show the other spouse as the beneficiary of the life insurance. Durable powers of attorney, designations of health care surrogate, and living wills should also be drawn up. Usually the primary decision maker is going to be the spouse. The secondary is often a parent or sibling.

Newly Married with Minor Children

When newly married couples decide to have children, a whole new estate game plan comes into play. For many couples, it will be the first time they think about what will happen to the child upon their death. Here the estate plan usually gets interesting. Who would be the best person to bring up your children? Do you trust the same person with handling the finances?

What I see many times is that the couple agrees that a person would be great to bring up the child, but they would not want that individual to have control over the child's money. Young couples in their late twenties and early thirties are usually just starting out and are many times worth more dead than alive. What I mean by this is they have a lot of life insurance that they received from work. I also counsel young couples that they should also look into the purchase of life insurance for each other and have enough money for the upbringing of their children.

Although the dynamics of today's family are changing, many times I find that one spouse has significantly higher income than the other does. If this is the case, the spouse with the higher income often believes that he or she should carry the life insurance and the other spouse would not require a policy. I believe that both spouses, if they have minor children, should have sufficient life insurance to provide lost income for the spouse and family. Even if one spouse is a stay-at-home parent, life insurance will still be needed to pay for a nanny or other childcare.

One way a young couple can get affordable insurance is to purchase term insurance, which enables the insured to pay a person a fixed amount of premiums per year for the term of the insurance. If the insured dies within the term, the insurance company pays the insurance to the beneficiary of the policy.

The problem with this insurance is that, upon the end of the term, all the money paid for the policy is wasted, and the person has nothing. Term insurance is usually very inexpensive and a good way for a young couple to have some protection and not spend a lot of money for it. The question then arises how they should structure the life insurance beneficiary designation.

If the young couple does not get sound estate planning advice, major problems can arise. For example, George and Mary, a young couple, have two small children, James and Michelle. George and Mary each took out life insurance policies for $750,000 of term insurance. If they pass away, they know they do not want their kids to have the money at age eighteen, so they make Mary's sister, Barbara, the secondary beneficiary of the life insurance policy. They believe that Barbara would use the money for James and Michelle.

Unfortunately, George and Mary were out on a date night when a hit-and-run driver killed both. The life insurance proceeds were paid to Barbara because she was the secondary beneficiary after George and Mary. Barbara used the money for two years for James and Michelle, but then she was then diagnosed with cancer and liquidated the account fighting her illness until she passed away. Her remaining estate then went to her husband, who decided to leave the country. With no surviving guardians, James and Michelle became wards of the state.

What George and Mary should have done was to make each other the primary beneficiary of their life insurance and a testamentary trust under their respective estates as the secondary beneficiary. This simple testamentary trust under their last will and testaments would have named a trustee of the trust and directed the funds to be distributed at an age they believed James and Michelle would be able to handle the money.

Having a will direct the assets does require probate administration on the life insurance proceeds, but I believe it is far better to go through probate and have the proceeds distributed to a trust than to enable children to own the funds outright.

Married With Newly Adult Children

Married couples with newly adult children can also have their own special challenges. Once a child reaches the age of eighteen, there is usually no need for guardianship unless the child has special needs. The question arises whether it is appropriate to now change the married couple's estate plan to enable the child to legally handle responsibility as the personal representative of their estates, trustee over their trusts, and medical and financial power of attorney.

Unfortunately, there is no hard-and-fast rule as to whether a child of eighteen should be put in charge. It is always on a case-by-case basis. Some children who are eighteen years of age are mature enough to easily manage their parents' affairs if required. On the other hand, there are a multitude of children who are over eighteen but are in no way mature enough to handle their parents' affairs. Some of the biggest changes happen in a child's life between the ages of eighteen and twenty-five. Parents should change their estate plan if the child has abused drugs or alcohol, gets married young, or has a rocky marriage.

If a child has been abusing drugs and alcohol, different protections can be placed in the parents' estate plans so the child must get tested before receiving any of the assets if the parents pass away. An experienced attorney can help draft an estate plan to protect the children from receiving the assets of their parents.

Married With Adult Children

Married couples with children aged twenty to thirty-five present other challenges. It is this time that a parent's estate plan should be reevaluated. In my experience, once a married couple's assets are more than $300,000, this is when clients should think about changing from simple wills and look into forming revocable living trusts. The married couple should likely have a full estate plan done. This estate plan should incorporate pour-over wills, a revocable living trust, durable powers of attorney, health-care surrogates, and living wills. It may be appropriate to have the adult child become the secondary trustee, personal representative, agent under a durable power of attorney, and health care surrogate.

If clients have multiple children, it is sometimes hard to choose which child should be in charge. This may be the hardest thing for clients to decide. Many parents do not want to hurt the feelings of one child by choosing another child to do important tasks. If a client has many children, I usually counsel against using two or more children to do these functions together. If a client chooses two children to be the trustees or power of attorney, then both will have to make the decision together. But if they do not agree, then nothing will be accomplished. Sometimes the only way to determine what is to be done is to let a court decide, which can become time consuming and costly.

If one child is more financially capable than the others are, he or she may be recommended as the secondary trustee and power of attorney. Another child may be geographically closer or in the medical field and may make a good successor health-care surrogate.

Another issue that frequently comes up is that an adult child marries a person who does not get along with the parents of the adult child. The parents would like to give their assets to the adult child if they were to pass away but not to the spouse of the adult child. Many times the parents would like to put a contingency into their estate plans, stating that if the adult child were to get a divorce, only then would he or she get an inheritance. However, in Florida, it is against public policy to encourage divorce in order to receive an inheritance, and a clause like that would not work in an estate plan.

What can a couple do to guarantee that only the adult child gets the inheritance and not the spouse of the adult child? This can be accomplished in several ways:

- To only give income from the trust to the child and not an outright distribution.
- To give the inherited assets to the child when he or she reaches a certain age further down the road, therefore giving the adult child time to see if the marriage survives the test of time.

Older Married Couples with Adult Children

When an adult couple is in their late sixties or older, many other challenges start to emerge. Health issues can begin to plague the older couple. Entering the twilight of one's life can be very difficult. The older couple has to deal with the fact that they are probably starting retirement from work, they are spending more time together than ever before, and their relationship may be changing from one of worrying about their children to beginning to be anxious about themselves.

Once a couple retires from work, they have to take a hard look at their estates to see what kind of budget they need to ensure that their money will not run out. While the couple was working, they were likely bringing in enough income that work income could make any expenditures. Once the couple retires, the only income that couples usually have are pensions, Social Security, and income from retirement plans. It is not uncommon for a couple to put themselves on a very strict budget when they retire. Adult children may see this budget as being cheap because the parents can no longer support the children without jeopardizing their own ability to pay for their expenses.

Another potential problem arises when one spouse has medical issues. The other spouse may then become the caregiver to the spouse who has these issues. The spouse who is now a caregiver may not be emotionally or physically ready to take on this responsibility.

Married with a Sick Spouse

Sometimes the unthinkable happens. A spouse becomes sick and can no longer be kept at home. At this time, a nursing home may be a good option. While many people would like to stay at home, the services needed to remain in a residence are very expensive and can very quickly eat away at a couple's savings. A stay at a quality nursing home may also be very expensive, at upward of $120,000 per year. Even a couple with substantial assets can find the cost of a nursing home to be outside of their budgets. What can the couple do? The answer can lie in extensive Medicaid planning.

Medicaid Planning

Medicaid is a health care program that assists low-income families or individuals in paying for long-term medical and custodial care costs. When a person receives Medicaid in a nursing home, the cost of the nursing home is completely paid for.

How can a person receive Medicaid? There are several qualifications. Medicaid Institutional Care Program (Medicaid ICP) pays for the majority of the cost of living in a nursing home. In order to qualify for the Medicaid ICP program, you must be sixty-five or over or disabled. You must also require assistance with activities of daily living (ADLs). There are six major ADLs:

1. **Bathing**—the ability to clean oneself and perform grooming activities like shaving and brushing teeth
2. **Dressing**—the ability to get dressed by oneself without struggling with buttons and zippers
3. **Eating**—the ability to feed oneself
4. **Transferring**—the ability to either walk or move oneself from a bed to a wheelchair and back again
5. **Toileting**—the ability to get on and off the toilet
6. **Continence**—the ability to control one's bladder and bowel functions

If a person can do all six ADLs, he or she is not considered in need of care and would not be able to qualify for Medicaid. If a person has great difficulty with only one out of the six ADLs, he or she would qualify for the lowest level of care, adult care, but still not qualify for Medicaid.

If a person is unable to perform two out of the six ADLs, he or she would qualify for a medium level of care, assisted living. If a person required assistance with three out of the six ADLs, his or her condition would be deemed to require a nursing facility level of care and qualify for Medicaid. A doctor's diagnosis of severe dementia will also qualify a person for Medicaid in a nursing home.

In Florida, Medicaid will only pay for those who need a nursing home level of care (three or more impaired ADLs). Those who require a lower level may be able to obtain assistance through a Medicaid waiver or Medicaid diversion program. The Florida Department of Elder Affairs representative will conduct a comprehensive assessment and review for long-term care services. This is also referred to as a CARES Assessment or the CARES Program.

The CARES Program is a prescreening program to review the level of care required for a nursing home resident or a person looking for home and community-based services (such as through the Adult Cystic Fibrosis Waiver, AIDS Care Waiver, Traumatic Brain Injury or Spinal Cord Injury Waiver, Familial Dysautonomia Waiver, or Florida Managed Care Long-Term Care Program). Once the Medicaid ICP program application is submitted, a CARES assessment will be triggered.

In order for a person to qualify for the Florida Medicaid program, an individual must also be a United States citizen or a legal resident and must reside in Florida.

Other Medicaid Qualifications

In order to qualify for Medicaid, it is not enough just to qualify medically. There are other major qualifications as well.

1. **Income Requirement**—The person's gross income must not exceed $2,205 per month.
2. **Assets Requirement**—The person's assets cannot exceed $2,000, and a couple's assets cannot exceed $120,900. The home is an exempt asset as long as the equity in the home does not exceed $560,000.

These are the figures for the year 2017 and often change each year. You will need to verify the current requirements before assessing if you meet the income and assets requirement.

Qualified Income Trust

Many clients come to my office with income that is greater than $2,205. The question is whether anything can be done so they still qualify for Medicaid if their income is greater than the $2,205. The answer is yes and relies on creating a qualified income trust (QIT).

If your income is over the limit to qualify for Medicaid, you can use a QIT to allow you to become eligible. You must place all your income into a trust account each month, and the trustee then transfers the income to the nursing home. The QIT involves creating a trust, setting up a special bank account, and making deposits into the account. Only a qualified attorney can set up this trust.

How do you set up a QIT agreement? A QIT must meet specific requirements and be approved by the Florida Department of Children and Families (DCF). A copy of the QIT agreement must be submitted to DCF for review and approval.

What items must be included in the QIT agreement? The QIT agreement must

1. be irrevocable (which means it cannot be changed or canceled);
2. require that the State of Florida receives all funds remaining in the trust at the time of a person's death (up to the amount of Medicaid benefits paid on the person's behalf);
3. consist of a person's income only without assets added or included; and
4. be signed and dated by the person or the agent for that person.

How does the QIT account work? After setting up the account, a person must make deposits into the QIT account every month for as long as the individual needs Medicaid. This means a person may need to make deposits before the Medicaid application is approved if he or she needs Medicaid coverage. A person needs to take great care to make monthly deposits because, if he or she fails to make a deposit in any given month or to deposit enough income, the person will be ineligible for Medicaid for that month. As long as an individual makes the deposits of income into the QIT account in the month it is received, it will not be counted when determining eligibility for Medicaid for that month.

What if you have assets over the $2,000 limit for an individual or $120,900 for the Community Spouse Resource allowance? What can you do to qualify for Medicaid? One approach would be to give

WHAT YOU NEED TO KNOW BEFORE YOU GO

away all your assets except for $2,000. This sounds like it may be a good plan, but there is a problem. Congress has included a look-back feature in its eligibility requirement. Any transfers made within five years of the application for Medicaid will be counted in the person's assets and not allow the individual to qualify for Medicaid. It is very difficult to know if a person will need Medicaid five years into the future. Also, many people do not want to give up their assets unless they know that they will be used only for a nursing home.

Personal Services Contract

One of the best methods for legally transferring assets and not have the assets looked at as a gift is to use the personal services contract—a formal, irrevocable written agreement or contract. Under Florida law, only a licensed attorney can draft this document. This agreement is between two or more people. The care provider (provider) agrees to provide personal, health-care, and/or managerial services to the elderly applicant or care recipient (recipient) in exchange for compensation paid by the recipient.

Under the personal services contract, the elderly applicant's assets are transferred to the provider in exchange for care management services that were provided by the provider for the lifetime of the recipient. The provider must treat the amount received as income.

In order for Medicaid to recognize this agreement, the contract must be irrevocable and assets must be transferred to the provider shortly after the contract is signed. Proof of the signed contract, asset transfer, and weekly logs must be submitted to Medicaid when applying for benefits.

How the Calculation of the Funds Sheltered Is Determined

Under a personal services contract, the recipient must determine a calculation of funds sheltered. This is based on a formula, which a number of factors calculate:

1. You must find the recipient's life expectancy in years, which the Social Security Period Life Table determines. The table is used by looking at the recipient's age and gender.
2. This life expectancy is then multiplied by the hours of services estimated to be performed by the provider, multiplied by fifty-two weeks a year, and multiplied by the rate per hour of the provider.

Who Should Sign the Personal Services Contract

The recipient and the provider must sign the personal services contract, and it must be notarized. An agent, under a durable power of attorney, may sign the personal services contract, provided that the power of attorney document has the proper language to allow a personal services contract. An experienced attorney should review a prior drafted durable power of attorney to see if it authorizes the signing of a personal services contract.

The provider must perform services listed in the personal services contract, for example:

- periodically assessing the personal needs and desires of the recipient as to social, physical, entertainment, hobby, personal hygiene, beauty maintenance, and other personal factors;
- regularly monitoring the physical, emotional, and mental condition and nutritional needs of the recipient in cooperation with health-care providers; and
- arranging for assessment, services, and treatment by appropriate health-care providers—including but not limited to

physicians, nurses, nurses' aides, nursing home services, physical therapists, and mental health specialists—to aid in diagnosis, treatment, palliation, cure, and remedy of the health, physical, and emotional status of the recipient as may be deemed necessary due to illness, discomfiture, or mental health, as is found to exist from time to time as well as many other duties.

The provider must keep a log of time spent each week for the services performed. The logs should be kept for the entire length of the personal-services contract starting on the date it is signed. The log document must state the dates of the services, type of service provided, and number of hours spent, and the provider must sign it. If the recipient is applying for Medicaid, the initial logs must be submitted with the Medicaid application for review by the Department of Children and Families.

Resources that can be transferred under the personal services contract are bank accounts, certificates of deposits, life insurance policies, annuities, stocks, and properties.

The personal services contract allows the elderly person needing benefits to prepay for services not covered by Medicaid and therefore increase his or her quality of life. The services to be provided are specified in the contract and should be in accordance with the recipient's needs.

The personal services contract is effective upon the date it is signed and ends when the recipient dies. The funds transferred to the provider remain in the provider's possession regardless of whether the recipient lives his or her full span or dies before or after his or her life span. Refunding the funds to the recipient estate would be a violation of Medicaid rules. The personal service contract is for the lifetime of the recipient, even if the recipient lives past the life expectancy of Social Security Period Life Table.

The following is an example of the personal services contract. John Worth is a single man and has assets of $250,000. He has recently been admitted to a nursing home in Florida. His son, James, has come into my office to see if John can qualify for Medicaid benefits. I told him we would be able to qualify his father for Medicaid. John is eighty-one years old, so we set up a personal services contract, which identified James Worth as the provider. Since John is eighty-one, based on the tables, his life expectancy is 7.41 years. This allows for services of approximately twenty hours per week at thirty-five dollars per hour. The math is as follows: 7.41 years × 20 hours × 52 weeks of the year × $35 per hour = $269,724. This is the amount that should be transferred to James Wayne under the contract.

Since John Worth does not have the full amount, the amount to be transferred would be $250,000, and if John were to receive any amounts in the future, those would also be transferred to James. The only downside to the transfer is that James will have to pay income taxes immediately on the $250,000 transferred, but John can show DCF that he has no assets and can qualify for Medicaid. John was mentally competent to sign, but we also had John sign a durable power of attorney with special Medicaid language so that if, in the future, he could not sign, then James would have full power to sign documents on his behalf.

Frequently Asked by Seniors

In talking to many clients, I find that they have many misconceptions about Medicaid. I believe it's important to set the record straight.

1. *Once I provide the attorney with the information he or she needs to complete the Medicaid application, how long does it take to be approved?* After completion of the required documentation, the attorney should make an application to the Department of Children and Families (DCF). It may take upward of sixty days to achieve approval. Unfortunately, there is no way to know how long DCF will take to process your application. Regardless of the amount of time it takes to gain approval, in most cases, the Medicaid coverage is retroactive to the month of eligibility.
2. *What is the five-year look-back period?* Under current law, DCF can review your finances for the past sixty months and assign a penalty period (expressed in terms of months of ineligibility) for large gifts you made during that time period.

3. *Am I required to have an attorney in order to protect assets or income?* Yes. Under the current Florida Supreme Court opinion, a non-attorney cannot assist or even give information about a person's particular Medicaid eligibility status and the availability of different asset protection plans.
4. *Will Medicaid take the homestead property?* No. In Florida, if the property is your homestead, it will be protected in most cases as long as you, your spouse, dependent children, or a disabled adult child lives in the home. The state does have the right to take the home upon the death of the Medicaid recipient, but this rarely happens.
5. *What is "Medicaid Pending"?* Some facilities may choose to allow their residents to move into their facilities and pay only their monthly income while they wait for the Medicaid ICP to be approved. Many of these facilities charge the full rate until the Medicaid ICP is approved.
6. *If a person moves out of Florida, can Medicaid benefits be transferred to another state?* Unfortunately, Medicaid benefits are not transferable from one state to another, so a new application is required.

The Top Five Myths about Florida Medicaid Qualification

1. *You have to give all your assets away or wait until you are impoverished in order to qualify for Florida Medicaid.* As we talked about before, some strategies can be used to legally restructure your

assets so you don't have to "spend down" your life savings and you can still qualify for Medicaid.
2. *Once you are in a nursing home, it is too late to start Florida Medicaid planning.* It is never too early or too late to begin Florida Medicaid planning. In those cases where planning was not done and the person is already in a nursing home, assets can still be protected. An attorney can use certain strategies to help you qualify for Medicaid in a short time frame.
3. *If you put all your money in your spouse's name, you will be eligible for Florida Medicaid.* Unfortunately, assets of both the spouse and the applicant are counted in determining financial eligibility.
4. *If you give away your assets, you won't be eligible for Florida Medicaid for three years.* DCF may look back at gifts made within five years.
5. *If a revocable living trust owns your assets, they are protected from nursing homes.* Assets owned by a living trust are still vulnerable to nursing homes' costs and are counted when determining Medicaid eligibility.

Once a person qualifies for Medicaid because he or she has no assets, his or her income is under the limit, and he or she cannot do three or more of the ADLs, then the person is ready to qualify for Medicaid. The next step can be very daunting for many people. That is doing the application itself.

If you are not familiar with the application process, it is very easy to make mistakes and have the application denied. I feel very strongly that the average person should hire an attorney to handle the application process. A qualified attorney can usually qualify a person for Medicaid within sixty days.

If a person is in an assisted-living facility, he or she can still qualify for Medicaid, but the process is a little different. The person should first be put on the Medicaid waiting list. This list is given to DCF and can take up to two years for approval. Once a person is listed, he or she has thirty days to qualify for Medicaid. Once qualified, he or she is entitled to up to $1,200 per month to be paid directly to the facility with his or her medical expenses paid.

Florida Homestead

Homestead in Florida is often very convoluted and strange to a person who moves to Florida from a state that does not have a homestead law. You must also reside in the home as your permanent residence. The three main functions of homestead property in Florida are real-estate taxes, creditor protection, and death, descent, and distribution.

Real-Estate Taxes

By qualifying your home for homestead, you gain certain exemptions from real-estate taxes. In order to qualify for homestead, you must have legal or beneficial title to a home on January 1 of that year. You must either apply for the homestead exemption in person at the property appraiser's office in the county where the home is located or go online. There may be some senior exemptions if you are sixty-five or older, depending on the county you live in. There are several personal exemptions, some of which are as follows:

1. **Widow or Widower Exemption:** If you are a widow or widower, you will receive a $500 exemption off your property value upon showing a death certificate of your spouse. If you remarry, you will no longer be entitled to this benefit. You must have been legally married to the deceased at the time of his or her death.
2. **Disability Exemption:** Every Florida resident who is totally and permanently disabled qualifies for a $500 exemption. When submitting an application, at least one of the following must be submitted as proof of your disability: a physician's certification of total and permanent disability prepared by a Florida physician using Form DR-416 or certificate from the US Department of Veterans Affairs.
3. **Blind Disability Exemption:** Every Florida resident who is blind qualifies for this $500 exemption. Any one of the following documents would confirm your claim: certificate

from the Division of Blind Services of the Department of Education, certificate from the United States Department of Veterans Affairs, certificate from the federal Social Security Administration, physician's certification of total and permanent disability prepared by a Florida physician using Form DR-416, or optometrist's certification of total and permanent disability using Form DR-416B. A blind person is defined as an individual having central vision acuity 20/200 or less in the better eye with correcting glasses or a disqualifying field defect in which the peripheral field has contracted to such an extent that the widest diameter or visual field subtends an angular distance no greater than twenty degrees.

A disabled veteran is any ex-service member who is a permanent resident of Florida and was disabled at least 10 percent in war or by service-connected disability. He or she is entitled to this $5,000 exemption. At least one of the following documents that provides the disability rating will evidence entitlement to this exemption: certificate from the US government, letter from Veteran's Affairs, or identification card from the Veteran's Affairs. Under certain circumstances, the benefit of this exemption can carry over to his or her spouse in the event of the veteran's death.

In 1933 the legislature began the Homestead Exemption to ease the burden of property taxes after the Great Depression of 1929. The initial exemption of $5,000 was approved and placed into the constitution in 1934, and it can currently be found in Article X, Section

7. The exemption was increased to $10,000 in the 1960s, again to $25,000 in the 1980s, and once more in 2008 to the current $50,000.

This works as follows: if you have a home worth $200,000, for property tax purposes, the home would only be taxed on $150,000. Please note that the first $25,000 is completely exempt from taxes, but the second $25,000 is not exempt from the school portion of property taxes.

One of the most significant benefit of the homestead exemption is the "Save Our Homes" cap of 3 percent on increases in the home's value for property taxes. This means that your home's assessed value can only increase up to 3 percent per year.

Another significant benefit of homestead is portability. This is a benefit if you are in your homestead and decide to purchase a new homestead. You are able to transfer the "Save Our Homes" reduction in the assessed value of your old home to your new residence so you continue to save on property taxes.

Creditor Protection

Homestead also provides for creditor protection. If someone has a judgment against you, the judgment holder cannot force you to sell your homestead in order to pay off the judgment. This protection is also available to your heirs upon your death.

Death, Descent, and Distribution

Homestead also relates to inheritance upon death. Upon your death, the distribution of your homestead property can get very complicated. The following are possible situations:

1. If you die with a spouse and no minor children, you can devise your homestead directly to your surviving spouse.
2. If you die owning a homestead property and are not survived by a spouse or minor children, then you can distribute the property to whomever you wish. You are free to disinherit a child and give the home to another child or anyone you want.
3. If you die survived by a spouse and a minor child but the homestead property was titled only in your name, then your spouse only receives a life estate in the property with the remainder interest going to your children in equal shares. The life estate interest means your spouse can live in the home for his or her lifetime, but he or she must pay for all expenses on the property, which include taxes, insurance, and other maintenance fees. Your spouse cannot force the children to sell the property, and the children cannot force your surviving spouse to sell the property. However, your surviving spouse can elect instead to receive half of the property as a tenant in common with your children instead of your surviving spouse having a life estate.
4. If you die and are survived by a spouse and own the home jointly with your spouse as "tenancy by the entireties," then your spouse will solely own the home.
5. If you die with a minor child but without a spouse, then the homestead must pass equally to all your children, both minors and adults. Minor guardianships may be needed for any minor children.

I have had numerous clients come to my office with the following problem. The client is married but estranged from his spouse and has homestead property titled in his name. He would like the property to go to his children upon his death and would like me to make this happen.

Unfortunately, unless he gets a divorce or had a prenuptial agreement, he cannot distribute the homestead property to his children without his estranged spouse having some control over the property, either as a life estate in the property or a 50 percent interest. Oftentimes the client then asks if I can transfer the property to his children now. I have explained that, unless his spouse joins in the transfer of the deed they create, even though the property is in his own name, any attempted transfer will be void and will not work. Even if the client tells me that he purchased the house with his money before he was married, it does not change the outcome. The client still cannot transfer the property alone.

Changing Family Dynamics (Second Marriages)

As an estate planning attorney for more than twenty-five years, it is my experience that the hardest estate plans are the ones that deal with second and third marriages and with couples who have children from previous marriages. Three main situations arise when dealing with multiple marriages:

1. A couple is in their second marriage, one of the spouses has children from a previous relationship, the children have

grown up with the stepparent, and the other spouse does not have his or her own children. This is usually the most straightforward estate plan. It is common in this situation that the couple treats all the children as if both were the biological children of both people, and the estate plan usually reflects that most, if not all, of the assets will be distributed to the one spouse's children. The couple can use a joint revocable living trust and place all the assets into the trust to avoid probate. They should also have pour-over wills that will give any assets that are not in the revocable living trust to be placed into the revocable living trust. The attorney who does the estate plan should be careful about who he or she uses as the personal representative of the will. Even though he or she might want to use his or her brother-in-law as the personal representative, the brother-in-law will be disqualified if he does not live in the state of Florida, since he is not a blood relative to the other spouse. The couple should also have durable powers of attorney, health care surrogates, and living wills.

2. Another situation is a little more difficult to plan. In this case, a couple is in their second marriage, each spouse has children from previous marriages, and the couple has one or more children from their current marriage. In most cases, a joint revocable living trust will still work to distribute the property. The attorney can use percentages to distribute the property on the death of both spouses. The percentages would be for each of the children. There may be some disagreements

between the couple as to who the proper person should be as successor trustee, but usually the couple can agree who they feel is competent enough to handle this function. It is also very important to note that if the couple decides to exclude one of the children from the estate plan, the attorney should use an omit clause in the trust. The omit clause should identify all the children and state that for reasons personal to the couple, they chose to omit the child. It is not good enough to simply exclude that child, because he or she can come back and argue that the couple intended to include them but forgot. The couple should also try to refrain from giving one dollar or another deliberately small amount to a child, since that gives the child a beneficial interest in the trust and makes it very hard for the trustee to close the estate if they refuse to sign a release for their inheritance.

3. Usually the hardest estate plan is for the relatively new second marriage with adult children from each spouse from other relationships. This can be very difficult to plan for because oftentimes the children do not get along with each other, and each spouse came into the marriage with his or her own assets. Things are a little easier if there is a prenuptial agreement in place, but if not, there can be significant challenges. Sometimes two separate trusts work, with each spouse giving his or her assets to his or her respective children upon the first death. There could still be an elective share issue, which I will address later. Also, the spouses might want a significant

amount of assets to go to the survivor when one spouse dies. In certain instances, the best plan is to set up three trusts, one for each spouse giving assets to his or her respective children and one trust with any joint assets owned by the couple. Usually the best person to appoint as trustee of the joint trust after both spouses are unable to serve is an attorney or bank. If the couple is healthy and most of their assets are in joint names, but they would like to give a significant amount of money to their respective children, they can set up a life insurance policy that can pay to the spouse's children an amount that the person feels is appropriate. A joint trust can be used for the remaining assets. Many times I recommend that this joint trust become irrevocable upon the death of the first spouse. This will allow the distribution upon the second death to be made to all the children equally or in the percentages that the couple agreed upon together.

Elective Share Issues

I think a little history lesson is appropriate before we dive into the world of the Florida elective share. Before 1975, there were things called dower and courtesy laws. The common law stated that a wife had a right (dower) to a third of the lands of her deceased husband, and the husband had a right (courtesy) to a life estate in all of the wife's real estate. In 1975 Florida abolished dower and courtesy and gave surviving spouses the right to what was called an "elective share" of the decedent's estate.

From 1975 to 1999, the elective share could be made only against probate assets. Before 1999, one spouse could form a revocable living trust and place assets into the trust. And when the spouse died, he or she could give these assets to anyone he or she chose, excluding the other spouse if he or she wished. In 1999 the Florida legislature substantially expanded the elective share laws so the surviving spouse could also take the elective share from non-probate assets; therefore a revocable living trust could no longer prevent a spouse from taking a share from the deceased spouse.

Currently the elective share is an amount equal to 30 percent of the elective estate. Florida Statute 732.2035 sets forth the property that enters into the elective estate calculation. This property includes the deceased spouse's probate estate, defined as "all property wherever located that is subject to estate administration in any state of the United States or in the District of Columbia."

Also included in the elective share calculation are the following:

- joint accounts
- POD accounts
- property held in joint tenancy and tenancy by the entireties (limited to decedent's interest in the property)
- revocable trusts
- certain irrevocable transfers (including transfers with retained rights to income or principal or retained rights to discretionary principal distributions)
- life insurance policies payable to someone other than the surviving spouse (includible value limited to decedent's interest in net cash surrender value immediately prior to death)
- pensions and retirement plans
- transfers made within one year of decedent's death
- irrevocable transfers to an elective share trust

And there are some others. As you can tell, the calculation of the elective share can be very complicated.

So why is understanding the elective share important? It usually comes up when discussing estate planning and second marriages. The couple might want to have assets going to their respective children, but they must consider that the surviving spouse would be entitled to 30 percent of the deceased spouse's assets. This may change the way the estate plan should be drawn up.

Sometimes a postnuptial agreement should be signed so the rights of both spouses are addressed. A postnuptial agreement is an agreement between the spouses on how their assets will be distributed upon a divorce or death. Once properly done, the children will be able to receive their inheritance without the surviving spouse's intervention.

Costs

Like any other professional service, a cost is associated with drawing up an estate plan. And the cost will often vary based on the experience level of the attorney. A less experienced attorney may charge lower fees but does not have the experience to understand all the nuances of making a comprehensive plan. A new attorney may make a plan that is way too complicated for what the client really needs. The actual implementation of the plan, when needed, makes the plan much more expensive in the long run than a simpler plan. Conversely, if a client were to go to a very experienced attorney, two things can occur. If the client goes to a medium or large firm, the price is usually very high to do the estate plan. If you go to a very senior attorney, the chance you take is that the attorney will have retired or passed away before you do, and your family will need to find another attorney to help them settle the estate.

I believe the best attorneys to do an estate plan typically have between fifteen and thirty-five years of experience and are either in a solo law firm or one that is considered small. You should make sure that the attorney you choose only concentrates on the area of wills, trusts, and probate. By doing this, you will be most likely to get the best attorney for your specific needs. You should also check to see the attorney's rating with Martindale-Hubbell and make sure the attorney is licensed in good standing with the Florida Bar.

Usually there are two ways in which attorneys bill their clients: by the hour or a flat billing structure. If you go to a medium or large law firm, you will usually be billed by the hour. It is my experience that attorneys in those firms will bill anywhere from $300 to $750 per hour for estate planning documents.

The more common approach to estate planning is to charge a flat rate for a total estate plan or perhaps simply a certain amount per document. I believe this is the preferred method for clients since they know exactly how much they will be charged for their estate plan.

Sometimes I see clients who have done their own last will and testament and revocable living trust. They use companies like Legal

Zoom and other legal form companies just to save money. I could spend the next twenty pages discussing the potential problems with doing your own estate plan, but I will just say that you get what you pay for. I tell clients to think about it this way. If you have a problem with your leg and are told you need surgery, you have a choice. You can do the surgery on yourself to save money or go to a doctor. I don't know anyone willing or capable of performing surgery on himself or herself just to save money.

When a probate of an estate needs to be done, the legislature believes that a non-attorney would not be competent enough to navigate through the probate process so they require an attorney to probate an estate. I feel very strongly that only a competent attorney should prepare your estate plan, even to do a simple last will and testament. The prices to do a competent estate plan—which should include pour-over wills, revocable living trusts, durable powers of attorney, health care surrogates, and living wills and also transfer real estate into the trust—will vary based on the attorney that you choose.

It is my experience that a plan including all these documents will range from a very low $1,100 on the low end to $20,000 or more if you have a complicated estate plan. In my practice, I typically charge anywhere from $1,500 to $20,000 to do an estate plan. The charges for individual documents also have a large range. To draft a simple will, some attorneys charge anywhere from $150 to $2,000. You should sit down with an attorney and find out his or her experience, along with what he or she believes you need, and what it will cost. And then you can decide if you are comfortable to proceed.

CONCLUSION

I have gone over the basics of estate planning, which includes information on what a last will and testament is, and how it is used in a estate plan. As you have learned, any asset transferred to a beneficiary under a last will and testament will go through the probate process. You have also learned that there are many ways to avoid the probate process and that the best one is the use of the revocable living trust and the superdeed. We also went over the other important documents that should be used with an estate plan—a durable power of attorney, a health care surrogate, and a living will.

The book went over the different types of estate plans for the various stages in a person and couple's life. We also went over a very important discussion on Medicaid qualifications so a person in a nursing home can qualify for Medicaid.

Throughout this book, I have tried to give you some important information on the basics of estate planning, probate administration, and Medicaid. It is my hope that you not only gained information on how the estate planning and administration process and Medicaid works but also have a call to action and actually make an estate plan for yourself. Knowing information and how it works without putting that into practice does no good. Please, for the sake of your family, friends, and charities, take some action. Hire a competent estate planning attorney. I am sure you will be very glad you did.

Please call my office at (954) 430-5644 or e-mail me at attorney@superdeed.com if you would like to speak with me about your own situation, and I would be happy to help you.

Gregory Ebenfeld, Esq.

GLOSSARY

ADL: Activities of daily living used to determine if a person is Medicaid qualified. There are six: bathing, dressing, eating, transferring, toileting, and continence.

ancillary administration: A probate administration in another state.

capital gains tax: A tax on capital gains. The profit realized on the sale of a noninventory asset. The most common capital gains are realized from the sale of stocks, bonds, precious metals, and property. Capital gains may be taxed at a lower tax rate than other income.

care provider: A person who will provide personal, healthcare, and/or managerial services to a person in a personal services contract.

care recipient: The person who will receive the care from the care provider who will provide services to the elderly person in a personal services contract.

CARES Program: Comprehensive Assessment and Review for Long-Term Care Services as determined by the Florida Department of Elder Affairs representative to qualify for Medicaid.

contingent beneficiaries: The people who will receive benefits if the primary beneficiary is deceased.

courtesy laws: Common law rights that a husband had in the property of his wife before 1975 in Florida.

descendant: A related person, such as your child or grandchild.

domicile: The state that a person treats as his or her permanent home.

dower laws: Common law rights that a wife had in the property of her husband before 1975 in Florida.

durable power of attorney: A document that stays in effect through incapacity that allows a person to handle financial matters for a person.

elective share: Allowing a surviving spouse to take assets from a deceased spouse estate in an amount that was not given through a will, trust, or other ways.

end-stage condition: A condition that is caused by injury, disease, or illness, which has resulted in severe and permanent deterioration, indicated by incapacity and complete physical dependency. To a reasonable degree of medical certainty, treatment of the irreversible condition would be medically ineffective.

estate planning: Preparing for the transfer of a person's wealth and assets after his or her death.

executor: Known in Florida as "personal representative." A term for a person who is responsible for making sure that any debts of the deceased are paid off and any remaining money or property is distributed according to the deceased's wishes.

Florida Declaration of Domicile: A form available at the offices of the clerk to help establish domicile in Florida.

Form 709: A form used to report taxable gifts to the Internal Revenue Service and allocates the lifetime use of generation-skipping transfer tax exemption.

formal administration: The name given to probate in Florida for estates that consist of assets over $75,000.

gift tax: A tax on the lifetime transfer of property by one individual to another while receiving nothing or less than full value in return.

guardian: A person who looks after and is legally responsible for someone who is unable to manage his or her own affairs, especially an incompetent or disabled person or a child whose parents have died.

Health care surrogate form: A document that allows a person (the surrogate) to handle health-care matters for someone who becomes incapacitated and is unable to handle his or her own health-care matters.

heir: A person legally entitled to the property of another on that person's death.

homestead: A person's permanent residence. Florida has generous homestead laws that protect owners of their permanent residence from claims by creditors and give exemptions.

intestate: When a person dies without a valid last will and testament.

joint tenancy with rights of survivorship: A type of concurrent property ownership in which co-owners have a right of survivorship, meaning that, if one owner dies, the owner's interest in the property will pass to the surviving owner or owners without the need for probate.

joint revocable trust: A revocable trust containing the estate plan for two people.

last will and testament: A legal document that communicates a person's final direction pertaining to his or her possessions and dependents.

life estate deed: The owner of a property (grantor) transfers the legal ownership and use of some type of real estate to be used by another person for the life of a particular person.

life insurance: Insurance that pays out a sum of money on the death of the insured.

living will: A document explaining if you want to be on life support if you fall terminally ill and will die shortly without life support.

Medicaid ICP: Medicaid Institutional Care Program, which pays for the cost of living in a nursing home.

Medicaid Pending: Receiving services before the Florida Department of Children and Families has approved the application for financial eligibility.

medical power of attorney: Another name for a health-care surrogate.

omit clause: A special clause in a last will and testament or trust that omits a member of family from the document.

persistent vegetative state: A permanent and irreversible condition of unconsciousness in which there is the absence of voluntary action or cognitive behavior of any kind or an inability to communicate or interact purposefully with the environment.

personal representative: A term for a person who is responsible for making sure that any debts of the deceased are paid off and any remaining money or property is distributed according to the deceased wishes.

Personal service contract: A formal contract or irrevocable written agreement for personal services to be performed.

POD: Payable on death. An arrangement between a bank or credit union and a client that designates beneficiaries to receive the assets in a client's account.

pour-over will: A last will and testament established by a person who has already set up a revocable trust so that, upon the person's death, all of his or her probate assets will be transferred—or "poured over"—to the trust.

probate: The court-supervised process of transferring ownership to property from a person who has died to his or her heirs or beneficiaries.

qualified income trust: A trust established in order to qualify for Medicaid if his or her income exceeds the allowable amount.

quit claim deed: A deed used to transfer property in a non-sale situation, such as a transfer of property between family members. This makes no assurance that the grantor actually has an ownership interest in a property. It merely states that, if the grantor does, he or she releases those ownership rights.

real-estate taxes: Taxes levied on the real value of property.

residuary clause: A clause in a last will and testament that disposes of any property that remains after satisfaction of all other gifts.

revocable trust: A trust document, the provisions of which the grantor (creator) can alter or cancel. During the life of the grantor, income earned may be distributed to the grantor, and after death, property may go to beneficiaries.

Rule against Perpetuities: The principle that no interest in property is valid unless it ends not later than 360 years. A trust in Florida cannot go on forever. The trust must end within 360 years of its creation.

self-proving affidavit: A form added to a last will and testament in which the person making the last will and testament (the testator) and his or her witnesses swear under oath that they have signed and witnessed the last will and testament. A notary public must oversee the swearing and signing.

separate writing: Allowing a person in Florida the ability to give tangible personal property on a separate paper.

simultaneous death clause: Occurs when two people die at or very near the same time, and at least one of them is entitled to part or all of the other's estate on his or her death.

successor trustee: The person who assumes control of the trust after the initial trustee dies or becomes unable to continue with his or her responsibilities.

summary administration (probate): The name given to probate in Florida for estates under $75,000 or occurred more than two years after death.

superdeed: Term coined by Gregory Ebenfeld for a deed that transfers property after the death of the grantor and allows the grantor to change the deed without the beneficiaries needing to sign.

tenancy by the entireties: A type of concurrent ownership between spouses in which the other spouse owns the entire asset at the death of one spouse.

tenants in common: A form of concurrent ownership, which, upon the death of the first person, the ownership is distributed to the estate of the deceased person.

term insurance: A type of life insurance that provides coverage for only a certain period of time or years.

terminal condition: A condition caused by injury, disease, or illness from which there is no reasonable medical probability of recovery and can be expected to cause death without treatment. The attending physician has reasonably determined that there can be no recovery from such condition and death is imminent without the application of life-prolonging procedures.

testamentary trust: A trust that is created under a last will and testament.

testator: A creator of a last will and testament (either male or female).

testatrix: A female creator of a last will and testament.

TOD: Transfer on death. An arrangement between a bank or credit union and a client that designates beneficiaries to receive the assets in a client's account.

trustee: The person who assumes initial control of a trust.

www.ingramcontent.com/pod-product-compliance
Lightning Source LLC
Chambersburg PA
CBHW070303230526
45470CB00002B/694